THE PLACE BEYOND

ROSEMARY ARGENTE

© Rosemary Argente 2017

All rights reserved under Copyrights, Designs and Patents Act 1988. No part of this book may be reproduced or transmitted in any form or by any means, electronic or mechanical, photocopying, recording or by any information storage and retrieval system, without permission in writing from Asaina Books or the Author.

First edition 2018

Editor: Chris Wallace

Cover photo: By Brian Sherman

Publishers: Asaina Books
Website: asainabooks.co.uk
Email: rosa@asainabooks.co.uk

Books by the same author:

Blantyre and Yawo Women
The Veil
The Promised Land - Companion to The Veil
Broken Temple
Praying Mantis
Difference
Share the Ride
Home From Home
Essays and Poetry
The Place Beyond
Caesar and Mapanga Homestead

Novels:
All Mine to Have
Farewell Sophomore
The Stream of Memory
A British Throne Scandal

Science Fiction:
Farewell to the Aeroplane

Booklets:
Journey of Discovery
Enduring Fountain - Health and Well-being
Katherine of the Wheel
Cooking With Asaina

An eastern monarch once charged his wise men to invent an aphorism to be ever in view, and which should be true and appropriate in all times and situations and they presented him with the words:

"*And this too, shall pass away.*"

Famous Statements, Speeches & Stories
of Abraham Lincoln

ACKNOWLEDGEMENTS

My sincere thanks are due to Chris Wallace for editing the manuscript, to Salma Khan and Izabela Brzezinska for sharing their researches and experiences on the Rhesus Factor; and to other persons too numerous to mention, transcending the cultures with whom I shared my existence, most of whom have now passed on, and to people I have met in more rent times for giving me much of their time in our discussions to share their personal views on the meaning of life. My thanks are also due to Ian Upton, David Duddle, Brian Sherman, and Mark Sherman for their invaluable help on my struggles with technology.

CONTENTS

INTRODUCTION 1
CHAPTER 1 4
CHAPTER 2 10
CHAPTER 3 14
CHAPTER 4 26
CHAPTER 5 30
CHAPTER 6 34
CHAPTER 7 45
CHAPTER 8 52
EPILOGUE 55

INTRODUCTION

The Place Beyond is a testimony of my personal experiences which include prophetic dreams, premonitions in music and lyrics, messages and intuitions. From my extensive researches I believe that my experiences are connected to the fact that my blood type is RhD Negative as explained in the Epilogue.

The Rhesus (RhD) Factor -

According to the Mayo Clinic Staff, the Rhesus (Rh) factor is an inherited protein found on the surface of red blood cells. if your blood has the protein D antigen, you are RhD Positive. If you do not have the D antigen, you will be RhD Negative.

Having RhD Negative blood type is not an illness and usually does not affect one's health. However, it can affect one's pregnancy and needs special care if one is Rh negative and the baby's father is Rh positive. But these factors were unavailable during the early 1950s when I had and lost my babies (see Epilogue, Immortal Infants). Since the early 1960s when science had discovered the Rh factor pregnant mothers are given the anti-D injection which rectifies the situation).

Nick Redfern's book, *Bloodlines of the Gods*, subtitled "Unravel the Mystery of the Human Blood Type to Reveal the Aliens Among Us." is an eye-opener to the understanding of RhD Negative blood. Although he pre-warns the reader that the information he has submitted is "controversial in the extreme", he asserts that we should look at the possibility that our history of the human race is incomplete and lacks key issues. Two other writers are equally intriguing: Jim Marrs, *Our Occulted History*; and Michael Tellinger's two books: *Stone Species of the Gods* and *African Temples of the Anunnaki*.

****

On dreams and dreaming -

Jung Carl Gustav (1875-1961), a Swiss psychiatrist and psychoanalyst founded analytical psychology and his work has been influential not only in psychiatry but also in anthropology, archaeology, literature, philosophy and religious studies. Gustav referred to dreaming as the collective unconscious. Tapping into this collective mind is a rich source of information, guidance and spiritual directives. Our attention generally follows the movement of our eyes, i.e. our consciousness is usually focused on whatever our eyes are looking at. If we want to focus our awareness on something that is non-visual we tend to de-focus our vision or close our eyes to help us concentrate. Our eyes instinctively look up to the left when we access our rational mind (mental body) and up to the right for the creative mind (causal body). This phenomenon is related to the rapid eye movements we make during REM - rapid eye movements in sleep, a kind of sleep that occurs at intervals during the night and is characterised by rapid eye movements, more dreaming and bodily movement, and faster pulse and breathing.

According to Gustav, dreams are a mixture of recall and creativity so our eyes constantly flicker when we dream. As our consciousness expands, we begin to use many tools and methods to heighten awareness and bring about understanding. One of the tools or methods is our dreams. Our nightly dreams become more significant on the path because the soul begins to use dreams as a means of communicating our progress. In other words, dream-work is dualistic in nature. It is a tool for ascension here on earth and a doorway to the mysteries of the universe.

Dreams emerge from the unconscious and occur in the Theta Brainwave state. In this state, we are open to receive insights and information from the subconscious. In the deeper state of Delta, our minds are passive and therefore can pick up cues from the energy of people, places, present day or future situations.

****

Ever since I was a child and over the years Dreams and dreaming, Music and Lyrics have played a vital role in my life. I have dreamed of symbolic messages concerning loved ones, of much sadness and in some instances of passing on. Some of the messages in my dreams, as in music and lyrics, have been about things in general, and others affecting political change; and some of the messages contained important aspects enabling the alleviation of disasters in a few instances.

In the premonitions where death was the content of the message, death had taken place within a few weeks, in others several months, while in some several years later, and in most instances, no matter how long it took, death was the outcome. A message of death, whether in a dream or music and lyrics, transformed me into an intense feeling of 'bereavement' and totally transposed me into a mood of weeping uncontrollably, no matter how hard I tried to fight it.

I translate the meaning of most dreams according to the effect it has upon me and to my understanding of the message held in them. I have recorded in a diary most of my dreams on most occurrences and this expose contains only those I consider suitable to share. To this day I have been guided by my dreams with a few exceptions.

In more recent years, I constantly dream of those who made an impact upon my life and have departed from this world; usually amid many other people I have never seen or met before - in cosmic peace, beautiful surroundings, wonder and respect for the future infinitely.

CHAPTER 1

Personal issues

1938 - The most significant dream -

I was then eight years old - it is said 8 is the number of perfection.

I GAZED TOWARDS THE WESTERN SKY. The time was 2:30 in the afternoon. Then I was attracted by the rapid dispersal of white clouds to reveal a clear blue sky, and gradually a picture emerged upon the whole of the clear blue sky. The picture resembled that of a scene as on a theatrical stage, a rostrum. The whole stage was flanked by a drape of full-length heavy velvet curtains in a texture of a rich *purple* hue - I had never seen the colour purple before, this was the first time and it was awesome!

Three wide lumber steps led to the rostrum and to the right of the stage seated was Mother Mary, robed in a simple flowing garment of white calico cascading from her shoulders to the ground covering her feet. Only her head and hands were visible. She was holding in her arms her son, Jesus. He was also dressed in simple white calico.

Somehow, I was transported to the stage in the sky and I became part of the scene. Mother Mary looked directly into my eyes and there was an assurance, a promise in her gaze, as if we shared that moment. I returned her gaze and we looked at each other for a while. Then she said:

"My son shall always protect you."

Just as suddenly as the picture had appeared in the sky it disappeared, I was transported back to earth, but I continued to look upon the blank space in the clear blue sky.

In the place where the picture of Mother Mary and her son, spread the Union Jack. After a few seconds the flag fell from the sky to the ground. Its colours of red, blue and white changed to pale green on a white background – only two colours. I picked it up and on it was written:

"There shall be a world war and Britain shall be the victor." A year after my dream World War 2 broke out (1939) – Britain and the Allies, were the victor.

The question in my mind has always been that: had I not been exposed to Christianity and the Union Jack in a British Protectorate where I was born and raised, would a dream of Jesus, followed by the Union Jack, have come to me? Why not Muhammed, Krishna, Buddha, Dalai Lama, Guru Nanak or any other deity?

I was baptised as a Roman Catholic when I was an infant and exposed to Jesus in Christianity. Since my dream, I have kept the image of Jesus as my "Big Brother" - not George Orwell's Big Brother, or the one that appears on Channel 4 TV – but a rescuer and comforter. I have often asked why?

My own answer is that I was a bullied, lonely child; and I needed someone to defend and protect me. Bullied children have no where to turn and they suffer fear mingled with shame. Since my dream of Jesus, bullying never bothered me, for in my childish mind I carried the conviction to those who bullied me:

"My Big Brother Jesus will get you!"

Since the dream, Jesus constantly stands slightly to my left side facing me, smiling, with kind, understanding, assuring eyes and this image has been a guide to my conscience throughout my life. I cannot erase this picture from my mind, nor do I wish to – it is when I temporarily remove this picture that I am not of good disposition and regret my actions to others and suffer much remorse.

Nor can I change the characteristic traits of his person: light skin, with long golden hair, intense blue eyes and garbed in Biblical dress. This was the image of Jesus Christ as impressed upon us by the Roman Catholic priests, and other Christian denominations, within a colonial context – and that was my first image of Jesus in my tender years. It is of common knowledge, not only to those who were exposed to Christianity, that Jesus was Yeshua, a Nazarene Jew, and it is highly unlikely he would have had the characteristic traits of a Caucasian, unless he was born as a European Jew after some Jews were exiled to Europe. However I have met some Christian people who believed that Jesus was Italian and was born in Rome.

Do the characteristic traits of your defender/mentor matter? Or that Jesus was presented as a Caucasian? The place where I was born and raised had been colonised by white men who saw it best to introduce and establish a 'white' God. Prejudice, locally known as 'colour bar', reigned supreme then.

God and Jesus have been and are constantly in my thoughts in all I do and my constant prayer has been "to be worthy of God." Who prepares a table before me in the presence of my adversaries? Who pulls me out of the bog when I have been pushed there or fallen into by my own foolishness? Who fills my cup to overflowing?

(See below Chapter 8, Major Rescuers.)

****

Analysis of the dream

Chapter 1 above

While I have experienced perhaps the worst trials and tribulations that may beset a person, I have also had a great life and in most instances I have been much privileged. The big question is: What has the dream of Jesus in 1938 meant to me throughout my life?

John 6:35 reads:

"And Jesus said unto them, I am the bread of life: he that cometh to Me shall never hunger; and he that believeth on Me shall never thirst."

I have always felt the presence of God and Yeshua ever with me and in this 'presence' my prayers are constituted. No matter how difficult a situation has been, over and over again throughout the years, there has always been someone or others who have assisted me to come out of the 'bog' I may have fallen into. And, I strongly believe in abiding by 'Time', the master of change or evolution.

I am a great believer in William Ernest Henley's poem, *Invictus,* in the two last lines of the last stanza: "I am the master of my fate. I am the captain of my soul," and that I am myself to a great extent responsible for my own actions (see chapter 6 below).

The best way I can explain this is to take chronologically excerpts from *Blantyre and Yawo Women* which describes the journey of my life and important events. Also, hopefully to assist the reader on to further reading if he or she so wishes.

In my prologue to *Blantyre and Yawo Women* I have indicated that at some point in our lives some rescuer comes along to lift us from a crisis and I have listed those who lifted me from the age of 4 weeks. In appropriate chapters I have also explained the bogs I had been pushed in or fallen into by my own foolishness.

My own foolishness is attributed to the fact that most of the problems I have had in my adult life have stemmed from my poor perception of the situation and my failure to discern the matter (as indicated in chapter 6 below). These are mistakes that most of us make through the journey of life but we all can be wise in hindsight.

Though over the years with much interest I had followed astrology: the movements and relative positions of celestial bodies interpreted as having an influence on human affairs and the natural world (much opposed by religious leaders!).

****

All humans are all the same in 'human nature' and share a common humanity in: thought, feeling, bodies and minds, yet unique. In other ways all are poles apart and no two people are truly alike, nor can they have the same experience in life, same perspective, the same mind. Even identical twins are unique in this respect.

On astrology, my interest lay mostly in the effect it is said astrology has on people's outlook in the 12 Zodiac signs, covering the calendar months. For the purposes of this exposé I recall two relevant signs only, Fire and Earth. Fire: Aries, Leo and Sagittarius. They tend to be dynamic, temperamental, physically very strong, intelligent and ready for action. Earth: Virgo, Taurus, and Capricorn. They are 'grounded' and down to earth, can be very emotional, practical, loyal and stable. The Zodiac writings clearly indicate that mixing Fire and Earth may lead to a personality clash.

Despite my foreknowledge of the above, and being under the sign of Capricorn myself, I became involved with two men both of whom belonged to the Fire sign. First I married an Aries character and the marriage ended in divorce (see *Blantyre and Yawo Women*, chapter 13, Double Wedding).

The second, my constant companion, was under the sign of Sagittarius. (see *Blantyre and Yawo Women*, chapter 20, Definitive Journey – The Court Rooms). Both led to personality clashes and into much trials and tribulations and I put these experiences down to *poor perception and lack of discernment o*n my part.

****

Premonition of the distant future -1939:

I WAS NINE YEARS OLD when I was gripped by some inexplicable sadness and deep grief. I cried incessantly, inconsolably for several days because I feared that all my family around me were to die. My parents were deeply concerned but there appeared to be no answer to this somewhat unfounded situation. They had planned a holiday to visit Salisbury, Southern Rhodesia (now Harare, Zimbabwe) leaving my brother and I under the care of our grandmother, Asaina. At the last minute, our parents decided to take me with them because of my condition. As we drove off I looked at my brother, who was to be left with our grandmother and I sensed "he was going to die before me," and to my tender mind probably while we were away.

As I write this now, my brother died 22 years ago; my mother died 18 years ago; and my father died 17 years and 6 months ago, I survived them. Furthermore, all of my parents siblings and their spouses; and all their contemporaries are now dead and gone, save one relative of my grandmother who is 100 plus years old (but since commencing this expose she passed away on 30/06/17); as are all my contemporaries save two cousins. Living are the younger generations, though a few of them have passed on.

CHAPTER 2

1962: A dream before my decision to leave my homeland:

I was sitting in a tiny white boat sailing away in a sea of black ink, destination unknown. I was facing the shore and sailing backwards, as it were. On the sandy shore stood a boy of about 8 years old; his black hair and the colouring of his skin was like that of my daughter; he was shading his eyes with his right hand and watching me sail away.

I interpreted this dream to mean: he was my baby who died in infancy – he would have been 8 years old at the time of the dream; and he was telling me not to turn my back on the children of my homeland.

My decision to leave my home country and live in Britain was to a large degree for personal reasons (see Premonition and Strong Conviction below) and also due to political reasons, particularly corruption in the police force that put a threat upon my life. This was instigated by my ex-partner, a 'constant companion' of twenty years, and his new partner. The latter wanted my property, wished to possess my home and they both hired corrupt members of the police on trumped up charges to put me in prison from where I would be taken and eliminated (see *Blantyre and Yawo Women*, chapter 20, Definitive Journey).

****

1965: Premonition and Strong Conviction

At this time I had a very strong conviction to make arrangements for the future and commenced by taking my daughter for secondary education in the United Kingdom. At the time I could not place the reasons for this strong conviction though they became apparent at a later date.

I believed that it was important for my daughter to become acclimatised to Britain, a new environment where we would eventually settle. Though not known to me then, the most important point was that a good number of her contemporaries were afflicted by AIDS (see below 1990-1: Trials and tribulations for Malawi).

My daughter escaped the above and on the whole, it was a move for the better for both of us, at least I believe that.

****

Political issues

Premonitions

The last part of my dream of 1938 (above) was connected to the very important issue of the Second World War which affected many people universally and it was a major political calamity.

1946: Case of the Goan Community of Malawi

I was sixteen when we went to a party at the home of Mrs Dalvi in Limbe. Mrs Dalvi was owner of a private primary school that taught excellent English. As the party was in full swing, there was a "Sing Song" (the usual thing in those days) and one Goan woman sung the song: *"I Know Why and So Do You"*, composed by Harry Warren and Mack Gordon, featured in the film Sun Valley Serenade, Glenn Miller's band (1941) - the black and white Hollywood movies of that era:

> *"Why do the robins sing in December*
>
> *Long before the Springtime is due?*
>
> *And Even though it's snowing, violets are growing*
>
> *I know why and so do you..."*

Everything about the singer and song transported me to that feeling of deep sadness but not 'bereavement' and found myself in deep sorrow (at the time I could not fathom this feeling of intense sadness till much later after many such experiences).

Many years later, under the Banda regime the entire Goan Community were arrested and imprisoned without trial (see

Blantyre and Yawo Women, chapter 18, Republic Status).

****

1958: A Dream about deposition of a leader

In my dream I saw Dr Hastings Banda, the new African leader for Malawi, badly injured and sitting in a little home-made wheel chair and trying to motivate the chair with his hands. Three days later, he and his followers were arrested and detained by the British colonial government; and a State of Emergency was declared by the Governor on 03 March 1958.

This was a consequence of the fact that when the prospective leader came to the country, he did not seek electoral means to form a government but instigated his thugs to engage in riots (see *Blantyre and Yawo Women* chapter 14, Arrival of Hastings Banda).

****

1990-1: Trials and tribulations for Malawi

I then lived in Oxford, England. For five days and nights I grieved intensely for no apparent reason. I could not eat and I could not sleep, like someone close to me had died. Soon after, the consequence was deaths from AIDS of many young people. This was followed by economic suffering in Malawi when the President and his followers had become utterly selfish to enhance their own personal wealth (see *Blantyre and Yawo Women*, chapter 20 Definitive Journey).

****

2006: Riga, Latvia

I was taken to Riga for a holiday by two lovely people, my daughter Lorna and Archie, her partner. In the tune: *Latuiesu,* I felt and grieved for the suffering of the Latvian under the Russian regime.

At the start of World War II in September 1939 with the German invasion of Poland, Latvia had already come under the Soviet sphere of influence under the provisions of the 1939 Molotov-Ribbentrop Pact with Nazi Germany. On 22 August 1996 the Latvian parliament adopted a declaration which stated that the Soviet occupation of Latvia in 1940 was a military occupation and an illegal incorporation.

CHAPTER 3

Premonitions in Music and Lyrics

1959: My Brother in the tune *Swedish Rhapsody:*

> *"We were waltzin' together to a dreamy melody*
> *When they called out "change partners"*
> *And you waltzed away from me ..."*

The best known piece of music in Sweden, published around 1906, described as fantasy on popular Swedish folk melodies, was composed by Alfven in 1903. The tune was playing at the Welcome Inn, a pub my brother owned and the tune transposed me into bereavement.

Though the waltz points to a dancing partner, others who surround our lives are partners each in their own role. My brother changed his occupation from an outstanding gifted mechanic/engineer to own a pub when and where he went from an excessive drinker to an alcoholic.

The irony was that he waltzed away from everyone, divorced by his wife, and he died a miserable wretch in 1995 at age of 62, after many years of trials and tribulations of his own making.

****

1963: A constant companion

When I first met him at his home he played a record on his radiogram, the song was composed and sung by Slim Whitman (1923-2013), an American country music and western music singer-songwriter and instrumentalist. He was known for his yodelling abilities and his smooth, high, three-octave-range voice. Genres: Country music, Folk music, and <u>Contemporary Christian music</u>. It was one of the tunes *Blue Eyes Crying in the Rain:*

> *"In the twilight I see her - I knew we'd never meet again."*

The tune and the words of the song transported me into deep sadness and that feeling of 'bereavement'.

At the time the meaning of my sadness and feeling of bereavement was baffling to me After 20 years of a great companionship, he met and was commandeered by a designing woman 42 years younger than himself. We never met again and he died twelve years later (1995) a miserable wretch at her hands.

****

1970: A message of the illness of my constant companion

In 1970 my constant companion had a cough that would not go away; unexplained breathlessness; loss of weight; chest and shoulder pains; unexplained tiredness and lack of energy. He totally refused to see a doctor but he was getting thinner and thinner and he weighed only 112 lbs..

I had a dream: I entered a room and there was a man sitting in a chair, I could not see his face as he had turned away to his right side, looking out of a window. Then another man entered the room, he had a gun and fired a shot which hit the man sitting in the chair. I rushed to the man in the chair, his left hand was touching the right side of his ribs, where the bullet had hit him. He turned his head, looked at me and I recognised my constant companion.

This dream worried and motivated me promptly to seek medical attention which was very difficult because he continued to refuse to see a doctor. Then I sought the help of a surgeon friend who asked if the sick man would have any objection to taking me to hospital. I pretended that I was ill then he took me to the hospital. Tactfully he was examined by my friend who said:

"You are not looking well and you seem to have lost a lot of weight. Lets see..."

He touched his forehead and felt his pulse and said he was running a temperature. Then he called a colleague and together they agreed that tests be carried out which they did comprising of spirometry test, X-rays, blood and other tests; and they found that he had lung cancer on his *right* lung.

My surgeon friend organised everything for a referral to Guys Hospital in London and *post haste* I made all the travel arrangements.

"Don't worry. You are in good hands", said the nurse as she took the patient's hand at Heathrow Airport where we were met by ambulance and driven to Guys Hospital.

At Guys the patient had a private room and was seen by a Doctor. I was with him every day during the day and went to a London suburb in the evenings to stay with friends. Tests were carried out every day by the doctor who each time requested me not to be present when he was speaking to or examining the patient.

At the end of a week the doctor came into the ward with a consultant, who preferred that I remained present when they were examining and speaking to the patient. The consultant told me that, my companion had to have surgery at the earliest. As soon as the doctors walked out of the room my companion broke down completely. I was positive and vehement as I told him not to worry and that he was in the best hands and that he would fully recover.

The surgery lasted for six hours and I was with him till nine at night. He pleaded with me to go home and to come back in the morning. When I arrived the next morning the consultant spoke to me in private and said that he had removed all the affected areas of the right middle lobectomy of the patient's lung. He went on to say that he preferred to tell the person closest to the patient rather than speak to the patient about his condition:

"I would like you to be present whenever I visit the patient."

The consultant went on that five years from the date of surgery may be a difficult time since one might want to do more than one should; and that it would take the same period of time to know of complete recovery. I was to arrange for X-rays to be taken and sent to the hospital every six months to enable him to monitor the patient's recovery; and that he wished to see him again after one month.

After discharge from the hospital we remained in England for a month for the final appointment with the consultant before we returned home to Malawi. As we were met at the airport I felt triumphant that we had beaten that terrible awesome shadow of `cancer' and I was positive about a sure and complete recovery.

After three years had passed since his surgery he had recovered remarkably well. In fact, he was in better health than he had ever been since I met him.

****

1972: The passing of Anganga Asaina

The year 1972 was sad. I visited *Anganga* (grandmother) at Queen Elizabeth Central Hospital. She hardly recognized me and was breathing heavily. The nursing sister told me to telephone the next morning about seven. That night, I suddenly awoke from sleep at ten minutes to one in the morning, gripped by a terrible sense of loss and bereavement. I could not sleep again. In the morning, when I telephoned the Hospital, the nurse confirmed that *Anganga* had passed on at one o'clock that morning.

****

1975: A very special person

In a tune that transported me to grieve deeply (not in a sense of bereavement):

A Summer Place Composed by Percy Faith, Max Steiner, initial release 1959:

> "There is a summer place ...
> Your arms reach out to me ...
> And my heart is free from all care ..."

Her heart was free from all care in the drug culture of the 1970s, which commenced in the 1960s. She first headed for Zambia, the country bordering Malawi but I had no idea where she was or how she was.

I decided to contact a Roman Catholic Bishop I knew in Zambia (Denis de Jong who had been born in Malawi and moved to Zambia). He promised that he would try to find her. He found her in prison in Zambia (for lack of entry visa) and he managed to establish some contact with her. Then she later travelled with friends through foreign lands and wherever she travelled to Denis listed a chain of help through other Catholic priests in the areas where she went. I was most fortunate as he constantly kept me posted about what she was doing and on my main concern 'her welfare'.

In one place she met with a car accident in which she broke her leg. Amid all the trials and tribulations over a number of years, she recovered well from all that to become a strong personality and a very caring person.

****

1980: A goodwill message from Asaina, my grandmother

When I emigrated to Britain, before I decided what I was going to do, I was invited to be companion to a titled lady in Egham, near Windsor. She was of German origin. A few weeks after I was there I became ill with something that looked like measles all over my body. I was very concerned that my face would forever be scarred though only one sore was on the upper cheek of the right side of my face. The lady called her family doctor.

Then I had a dream. Asaina stood at the foot of my bed as she was at age 38 years (she had become a grandmother at 35). Both her arms were raised and she was holding on each of her palms an enamel plate with an assortment of wild fruit, the kind I used to pick when I was a child in Malawi (before man's rape of nature). The most remarkable thing was the clearness of the skin of her beautiful young face, without a blemish. She was smiling at me though she said nothing.

My interpretation of this dream was that I was not to worry about my face as it would not be affected or scarred in any way. I recovered well.

The other significant point was that because of the upset caused by the emigration from my homeland, getting something like shingles was a natural reaction. The one sore on the upper cheek of the right side of my face gradually became larger but feint in colour as the years went by.

****

1981-1992: Dancing Skeletons of Oxford

When I lived in Oxford I often went to Tea Dances at the beautiful Town Hall to the music of a live band. The floor was large, the dances commenced at 3:00 pm and ended at 6:00 pm.

On one of the days I sat out a number to rest and I had a vision which later proved to be about myself as it manifested in my twilight years. As I watched the other dancers swaying to the sound of the music they all turned into skeletons in their birthday suits wearing only one item, a pair of dancing shoes, dancing away...

I later moved to Bolton (where I lived for 18 years) and on one occasion when I was about 70 years old, I visited a podiatrist and she said to me:

"You are literally walking on bones!"

After this announcement I began to think seriously about my dream of the Oxford dancing skeletons and this is how I interpreted the dream:

After we die we become skeletons but usually not in our life time but in my dream I was not part of the dancers, I had sat out that particular number; and the comment "You are literally walking on bones" signified a 'living' skeleton.

Then while still living in Bolton, with a friend I visited London and along the way we stopped at Oxford and went to visit St Ebbes, where I had lived (see *Blantyre and Yawo Women*, Chapter 20, Definitive Journey). The people I had known, my contemporaries of the Tea Dances, all were dead and gone.

In my twilight years I moved to Dumfries and this is the point of my vision of the Dancing Skeletons. Osteoarthritis came upon me with a vengeance. I recalled an old woman when I was a child in my grandmother's village, who when asked how she was, said 'nyamakazi' (a form of rheumatism) travelled about her bones. I then thought what a cranky thing to say, how can anything travel in your bones... now I know what she meant - I am a walking skeleton. Sometimes, as a joke, I ask the GP's "any chance of a replacement skeleton?"

****

1986: Cat and Mouse Game With the Police

When I was under false imprisonment spanning over two years I let my residence at Mapanga to an English couple and moved to my parents home for safety. I cannot pretend that I was not frightened in my predicament. Every morning at 3:00 I woke up gripped by a terrible fear that almost chocked me. I took slow deep breathing exercises and by 5:00 am the fear eased, enabling me to get ready for a new day.

My fear did not deter me from my daily living and I defied the police and moved about freely. My father was concerned about my personal security and assigned to me a well trained bodyguard who accompanied me wherever I went, as I played a cat and mouse game with the police.

One morning I woke up with the premonition that the police would seek to re-arrest me on that morning. I got ready early and I left the house at 6:00 am. Before I left I requested my mother that should the police call she was to tell them that I had gone to Chileka Airport to catch a plane for Lilongwe. But I drove to Lilongwe via the long route of Zomba. Sure enough half an hour after I left two policemen were there looking for me. They went to Chileka Airport on a wild goose chase...

****

1986: Born Again experience

While in Lilongwe I met Rachel, a woman at a church my host attended. Rachel asked me if I believed in Jesus and whether I had been born again. My reply was that I believed in Jesus since I was eight but did not quite understand what was meant to be born again.

We agreed a date and a time to meet at the home of my host where Rachel explained that "Born Again" was a phrase used by many Protestants to describe the phenomenon of gaining faith in Jesus Christ. This was an experience when everything one had been taught as a Christian became real, and developed a direct and personal relationship with God.

We went through a session of prayer and at some point I felt a very strong 'presence'. So intense was the feeling that my chest was burning until I broke into uncontrollable flow of hot tears.

Sadly, I never discovered who the woman was despite my efforts to find and know her or where she came from – to this day she remains a 'mystery'.

****

1994: A cousin

I often visited my cousin in Knaresborough. On one of the visits she had a 45 RPM (revolutions per minute, denoting the speed at which a turntable should be) in music, a single or record single, a type of release, typically a song recording of fewer tracks than an LP record, an album or an EP record. It was Abba's tune *Chiquitita* that transported me to deep sadness (not bereavement) when I looked at my cousin while the tune was playing:

> *Chiquitita, tell me what's wrong*
> *You're enhanced by your own sorrow...*
> *Try once more like you did before*
> *Sing a new song, Chiquitita...*

She suffered severe trials and tribulations and left her beautiful home in England to make a new life in the Caribbean. She met with success to own another beautiful home and a large beautiful garden – she sang a new song.

****

1995: My Mother

In the tune of a Yawo song, played by the Malawi Police Band:

"*Wa janje, eh*". Meaning "answer them."

There was not much meaning in the words but the tune brought an intense feeling, which transported me into deep sadness and that feeling of bereavement. A few years later my mother suffered a broken hip and became bed-ridden for the last three years of her life. It was a time of loneliness, sadness and much suffering for her. She died in 1999 (see *Blantyre and Yawo Women*, chapter 22, Twenty-first Century).

****

1995: A constant companion

I dreamed that I was walking on a dirt road in an area that looked like a farm and I met my constant companion sitting on what looked like a farm cart. We were parted for 12 years and at the time he was with his new partner. In the dream he said to me:

> "*I am so sorry. Please forgive me. It was not 'my doing' for all the terrible
> things that were done to you*".

One week later I received a letter (those were the postal days before the advent of emails!) from the auditors advising me that he had died on 28/08/95, on the day of the night I had the dream.

****

2000: Roxanne, my niece

I visited my niece at her home in Malawi where her little nephew Jerome was also visiting with his mother. She played on her record player an LP with the tune *"Smoke Gets in Your Eyes"* composed by Jerome Kern (1885-1945) performed by the Platters:

> *"They asked me how I knew my true love was true...*
> *Something here inside cannot be denied...*
> *When a lovely flame dies*
> *Smoke Gets in Your Eyes"*

When I looked at my niece, the message of bereavement gripped me and I excused myself to the bathroom to cry in private. She had a divorce and with her two daughters she moved to the UK. I put this down to the sad message but I was wrong because the bereavement (in the messages I receive) meant 'passing on'. In 2010 she died suddenly of a brain haemorrhage at the tender age of 48.

The person who suffered the most was her partner whom she had met in England. When his mother had heard that he met her, she had said:

"I would like to meet the woman who has made my son smile at last."

Despite her family's efforts, he became a recluse, suffered an illness from which he had no desire to be cured. He never recovered from her death, my message after all included him - smoke got in his eyes. A broken man, body and soul, he died towards the end of 2017.

****

2012: A message of illness for a special friend

When I lived in Bolton I looked at a friend and in her face I saw, particularly the area surrounding her eyes, they were covered by some inexplicable shadow. I was filled with intense sadness but there was no feeling of 'bereavement'. I also noticed she had lost weight and I implored her to see a doctor.

It was discovered that she had cancer for a second time in a different part of her body. She recovered well.

We all have cancer cells. They lie dormant until they have been triggered by something which, in most cases, has to do with diet and lifestyle, according to my experience. Unfortunately, we do not have much choice on the foods we buy unless we make a point of constantly to check on our diet and change our lifestyle (see *Enduring Fountain – Health and Well-being*).

****

January 25-31, 2012 – visit to Belfast:
The prophesy of four

During my first visit to Belfast, Northern Ireland with a friend, four people, one woman and three men, total strangers, prophesied the same thing at different times:

> *"You have done, you are doing, and shall do even greater things for the*
> *children of your country but you shall not live to see the fruits of your*
> *labours."*

****

2014: Flossie, A special friend

At her invitation I visited her in Dar es Salaam, Tanzania, March-April. During this time together we visited what used to be the Slave Market at Zanzibar and shared the terrible experience of deep sadness felt by most visitors at the place. On return to her home in Dar-es-Salaam the following tune in Swahili played in her house a few days before my return home to England:

Unikumbuke: "Lord remember me when you are blessing others."

The now familiar intense premonition of what was to come was in that tune and the words as I looked at her. I excused myself to cry in private, deeply grieved. One month after my departure from there, on 09/04/14, my special friend died suddenly – cause of death was unknown.

The President of the country had her body lie in state for two days and repatriated her remains in his private jet to her home country Malawi.

This was a position she had earned herself; for she was known as the "Queen of Peace".

****

CHAPTER 4

Places:

1967: Shire River – Malawi

A friend and I visited a narrow part of the river with the intention to have a picnic. We could not stay as we felt so uncomfortable and I was filled with an intense feeling of bereavement. We did not have the picnic but departed from the place *post-haste.*

I later discovered that 250 Malawian slaves were killed when they were attempting to escape by crossing the narrow part of the river, in the mid-1880s. This was before the arrival to the area of Dr David Livingstone, the Scottish explorer, whose efforts led to the elimination of the slave trade replacing it with Commerce and Christianity.

****

1967 Chiradzulu – Malawi

We went for an outing to have a picnic on the top of Chiradzulu Mountain but we could not stay and had the 'imperative' feeling immediately to leave the place. The place had a grave sinister atmosphere. Later I discovered that 170 Malawian slaves were killed, during gunfire between Dr Livingstone and missionaries against the slavers, in 1889, in defence of the slaves.

****

1990: West Virginia, USA

I passed through West Virginia during my visit to Washington, DC. I was filled with the now familiar feeling of intense sadness. I later discovered that I had passed through a place where slaves worked in the cotton fields. Most probably some of them came from my homeland, Maravi, what later became Nyasaland, now Malawi.

The earliest arrival of slaves was in the counties of the Shenandoah Valley where prominent Virginian families built houses on their plantations. The western part of Virginia which became West Virginia was settled in two directions, north to south from Pennsylvania, Maryland, and New Jersey and from east to west from eastern Virginia and North Carolina.

****

2000: A dream of my mother in Bolton

It was a time of much loneliness for me when I met and became acquainted with a certain group of people. I dreamed of my mother who had been dead for a year. She was standing in a crowd in a town I had never been to before. She was wearing a red dressing gown. I walked towards her but as I was about to approach her she turned round and was walking away from me. I followed her through the crowd but she disappeared. I asked the people around if they had seen a woman in a red dressing gown, some shook their heads and others said she had walked on ahead but had disappeared into the crowd.

When I awoke from that dream I could not get the message she was delivering to me until a little later when I discovered that the people I frequented with were such that I should not continue with them. The colour of my mother's dressing gown was 'red' which spelt danger. After trials and tribulations with the group of people, and as a friend put it I had a "lucky escape", somehow by the exercise of diplomacy.

****

The Black Widow and the Egyptian Tomb

I WAS SITTING BEHIND THE WHEEL OF RUBY my car and found myself in her yard. I had driven there for some unknown reason. It was lunchtime when, I imagined, they would be having a refreshment break. I saw his car parked at the side of the abode. The outline of the abode was not quite clear but through an open door of what appeared to be a side door of the abode I could see through into the ante chamber somewhat resembling an Egyptian tomb. I saw her, the black widow, through the open door and she was standing within the ante chamber. She was smartly dressed in a cotton ensemble made from a print of orange and black colours.

The hem of her skirt was trimmed in black. She was arrogant. I seemed to have the power to read her thoughts and to know obscured facts. She looked hard at me and I read her thoughts as daring me to enter the ante chamber so she could "deal" with me. I also had the knowledge that although his car was parked at the side of the tomb he was not within the ante chamber.

In the realisation of great danger, I refrained from entering at all, and was gripped by the impulse to retreat as quickly as possible. As I reversed Ruby, I saw a man who was posing as her gardener, weeding in a squatting posture in a cheerless garden. I knew he was her sorcerer as he was observing me very closely. Although the windows of Ruby were closed and the man was speaking softly, I heard him warn three other sorcerers who were concealed in sugar cane bushes nearby:

"There she is retreating – let's get her!"

By then I had got Ruby into first gear. I saw through Ruby's rear mirror the concealed sorcerers coming forward out of the sugar cane bushes and joined the first sorcerer in their chase of me. I pressed my foot on the accelerator with all my might. Suddenly I was surrounded by a thick wood, ominous around me, it was as if the trees were closing in on me conspiring with black widow and yet I was not afraid. As thick as the wood was I could see the road ahead but I had to weave through the trees as they converged pressing towards me. I realised I could not make my escape through the road as the sorcerers had their hands stretched out towards Ruby.

I prayed that I should fly. With all my strength I held on to Ruby's steering wheel:

"Fly, Ruby! Fly!" I implored as I pressed on the accelerator. Then, just in the nick of time, Ruby soared up, up and away above the

tree tops from where I could see I was blocked by a huge mountain but I realised that the power of black widow and her sorcerers was confined to the ground.

Flight was my only escape. I held on the steering wheel stronger than ever and pressed my foot on the accelerator; and then Ruby appeared to possess renewed vigour, while I, realising that only my own strong conviction and determination would help me to escape. Ruby ascended and gained the top of the mountain. I woke up and looked at my watch. The time was 1:45 pm. I had been asleep for 45 minutes! This dream helped me to become vigilant during a time of great trials and tribulations when my constant companion had been commandeered by the designing woman in the Egyptian tomb.

****

CHAPTER 5

A Wake Up Call

Diary 2013

Monday 18 March -

"Can you manage the stairs to the plane?", the ground hostess asked me.

Sitting in the wheelchair, I replied "No".

"That's alright", replied the hostess. The carer pushing the wheel chair headed for the lift but it was out of order. He was obliged to find another route which took us outside of the terminal building to the aeroplane. There the wheelchair, with me sitting on it, was placed on a lift which hoisted us to a door leading on to the pilot's cabin to the right and the way to the passenger seats on the left.

I had told no one that all of a sudden I had lost the use of my body, a kind of semi-paralysis, though my mind was alert. I resolved to proceed on the flight to Malawi anyway.

All of the officials I came into contact with were most helpful and caring, I could not praise them enough. I felt a deep compassion for them in view of the somewhat scanty facilities which we experience in modern times because of cuts, redundancies, such as the failure of the lifts but these carers behind the scenes were totally dedicated.

When we use public facilities we take it all for granted and haven't the slightest clue as to what those behind the scenes do for our comforts and security during travel. Throughout my long journey changing aeroplanes in three cities during a total of 25 hours from departure door to destination door, and a total of 11 hours of actual flying, I was passed on from carer to carer.

For my part, I interpret this as a premonition of what may happen towards the last days of my life; and I take the partial paralysis, before I boarded the plane for Malawi, to mean that my body would cease to function before I was clinically dead at the time of my departure for the place beyond (see chapter 7, October 2016: The passing of Helen, a special friend.)

****

Tuesday, 19 March, 2013

At my destination, according to medical tests, the cause of the sudden semi-paralysis was said to be a reduction of white blood cells. I was given a course of antibiotics which somewhat improved my health but I remained inexplicably fatigued.

On my return to England, after appropriate tests were carried out, the medics confirmed that I had severe Vitamin D deficiency, but for some inexplicable reason, despite my stay of six weeks in the sun of Africa the situation had not improved while I was there.

I believe that this was a premonition as to what might happen should the failure of my body precede the departure of my soul from planet Earth.

****

Wednesday, 27 March, 2013

Dream of my father

On the ninth day after my arrival at my destination, I took my usual afternoon siesta and had dream: I was sitting totally nude in a room, huddled, covering myself with my arms, head bowed in a kneeling posture, when a door on the left opened and my father, who had passed on thirteen years ago, walked in and asked:

"Are you coming?"

I raised my head and replied:

"Yes, I am coming".

"Are you ready?" he asked again.

"I am getting ready. I am coming" I replied.

He then turned round, walked away and disappeared through the same door he had entered.

A friend's spiritual interpretation of this dream:

The fact that I was sitting in total nakedness signified that all wordily things had been stripped away from me, that I was exposed to my innocence, and that I was sanctified from earthly things. The fact was it was my Father, represented God. The door was a sign of transition into another world or dimension, namely Heaven.

The calling "Are you ready?" was a question from God of my willingness to follow the Almighty, now.

The next question my father had asked was:

"Are you coming?" which was an answer to the first question which was:

"Yes", I was ready" and "Yes, I was coming."

This was a wonderful confirmation of the building up of my faith over my life time, coming to fruition. It also brought joy to know that it was my Dad representing Father God. This is how my Christian friend interpreted the dream.

While accepting the above interpretation with due respect, my own personal interpretation was that: my father was giving me a message that as a precautionary measure I should prepare myself in the event of my becoming *non compos mentis* (not of sound mind) or in the event of my demise and to ensure there were trustees to take care of the situation. This dream strengthened my conviction to prepare a Settlement Trust.

****

Monday, 01 April, 2013 - A dream of passing on

I woke up at five (it is said 5 is the number of Grace) o'clock in the morning, unable to sleep for a while, then fell asleep again and had another dream:

I stood in a room facing Lorna and Archie, they were sitting, huddled, heads bowed and they were both crying. My daughter, Lorna was singing a heavenly song I had never heard before, like a hymn, in tune and lyrics beautiful beyond description. Then she lifted her face as if to look at me but there was no recognition in her eyes: I could see them but they could not see me – I was standing there in spirit, I had just passed on.

They were surrounded by Gladioli but without flowers on them only many tubers around – seeds? What seeds can be sown?

After these two dreams and before my departure for my home in Britain, I drafted a Trust document - as a way of 'getting ready' - in which I appointed two trustees in Malawi; and myself and my daughter as the other trustees in Britain. This was to continue in my work for the benefit of children (as the 8-year old boy had signified in my earlier dream), the members of my immediate family, and the elderly of Malawi, my home country, and other people in need elsewhere.

This dream gave me a message for something that was constantly worrying me. As so many of my loved ones had passed on, I always feared the passing on of Lorna or Archie before me and this dream gave me some degree of assurance that I should not entertain such a thought. It was most likely that I shall precede them to the place beyond. This is my hope in my prayers.

****

CHAPTER 6

A personal view of God

WHEN I AM ALONE I AM NEVER LONELY but unafraid and I feel the presence of God and Yeshua ever with me. It is my personal belief that God is everywhere and fills even the atmosphere. God is an abstract being, a spirit, and as such the spiritual side of each one of us is part of God. I think and try to live in God in all I do and seek to be worthy of the Almighty. God is neither male nor female. Therefore I prefer to use 'Almighty' as a pronoun of God, I cannot help the structure of the English language. To be worthy of God is; *"do to others as I would wish them to do to me."*

My constant thoughts of God and Yeshua are my prayers and I would not pray for foolish things such as long life for I am a mortal being and death knows no measure of time. For this reason I live each day as if it were my last and do my duties accordingly. I accept my own death without question, in fact with euphoria, though the death of others, particularly loved ones, strikes terror in my heart. It is hard to accept the death of others even though I know that death is inescapable. I believe that we do not die but transfer to another realm. Only the body dies. I believe that death is the end of the existence of my body, its place is Planet Earth, a place of death and decay. Because body was created not to last forever, it cannot continue to function, but death is not the ultimate end of my life. Death is the gateway to a continuation in the Spiritual Sphere – *the place beyond.*

When I am asleep, it is only my physical body that rests to awaken to renewed vigour; my spirit disengages itself and goes somewhere, I do not know where but I dream of places I had never been to where I meet people I had never seen before – usually in peace and friendliness.

The human is a triune being: spirit, body and soul (or mind), woven into the mystery and essence of our being, as the image of the supreme designer. The Spirit is boundless, endless.

The spirit is not within the body but an external light without the body attached to the soul within and hovers a human being from conception to death. The body is the tabernacle or temple that houses the soul; and body and soul make a dual consciousness from infancy to adulthood. The body simplifies our transit on earth, truly I am a brief tenant of this earth: billions of years passed before I was born and billions more shall pass after my death.

Good and bad are boundless conditions but may exist in "thought forms", long after the doers have passed on. Example: if you enter a building or visit a place you would sense the good deeds of the past. So too, where misery or persecution took place you would sense them, though not everyone experiences this. This means the inhabitants of buildings or places make 'thought forms' which inhabit the walls of the building or place: good or bad forms which are touched by the sixth sense. But most importantly, for the living, the legacy of the departed ones is of much influence to contemporary beings in varying degrees.

I consider a church, mosque or any other place of worship as symbolic to a particular kind of culture within that society and not that God is found in designated places of worship. It is not only prayer at a particular place of worship that leads man to the path of righteousness but to do no harm to any one. A person who spent much time at a place of worship but carried out evil deeds could not be exonerated from such conduct because of attendance at a place of worship. Any conduct that causes suffering to anyone upsets the equilibrium and as such could not be a blessing.

The prophets of God are as varied as the religions of nations, followed by the kind of faith and mode of worship from society to society as the cultures of this world. During life on earth a prophet may give spiritual guidance, achieved through faith. Therefore, I believe that God is not concerned with an individual's kind of faith. God as a supreme being gives justice to all.

By justice I do not mean heaven or hell hereafter. The court of the justice of God is within us. As the essence of justice, the Almighty, the supreme being cannot show mercy to one and not to another;

for that would be a denial of justice. All people were created by the one and same God, and God cannot deny justice because the Almighty carries no prejudice based on different faiths – in the belief that God is love, truth, grace, charity, peace, and justice.

Since we were made in the image of God, according to the Bible, we ourselves should take responsibility towards our fellow man. The first is bear no grudge against anyone no matter what they have done to you, hence the need to forgive does not arise. That would be a usurpation of the power of God and forgiveness belongs to God.

In Matthew 5:38 (New International Version of the Bible) on "Eye for Eye" Jesus said:

"You have heard that it was said, 'Eye for eye, and tooth for tooth. But I tell you, do not resist an evil person. If anyone slaps you in the right cheek, turn to them the other cheek also..."

I personally would prefer to walk away from the situation rather than have my other cheek slapped as well!

What we should carry in our heart is the words: "Do unto others as you would have them do unto you" taken from the words of Jesus in the Sermon on the Mount:

"All things whatsoever ye would that men should do to you, do ye even so to them", referred to as the "Golden Rule" and this is the sum of the law. In the Mosaic law:

"Whatever is hurtful to you, do not do to any other person" - Matthew 7:12 (NCV).

In adverse situations, the first thing to remember is: a *blessing* to you but a *curse* upon the one who has done it; forgive immediately and pray for them. Adverse situations are learning experiences.

While others shun all forms of religion some indulge in criticism of the faiths of others. They speak of God as if the Almighty was a piece of merchandise that called for a preference to a particular brand. What does it matter which is our or what we call God? What does it matter how God is worshipped if it brings comfort to the worshipper? For that matter an atheist could find comfort in non-worship. Entering a church with one's hat on instead of shoes off are but cultural norms and no one religion holds the key to heaven. The varieties of religions are learned culture which speeds the believers through daily life and in contact with fellow beings. But there are some who may rise above learned culture and see for themselves.

The presence or existence of God can neither be proved nor disproved and as such each individual has the right to believe in the way they feel or see. But in everything there is a corresponding state of quality: night and day; good and bad; weak and strong and so on. There is also a corresponding side of God: Satan represents all that is evil while God represents all that is good. No matter how powerful Satan may be in a particular set of circumstances, God will prevail in the end: because Godliness lies in the indestructible qualities of love, truth, grace, charity, peace, and justice.

However, these eternal indestructible qualities call for definition:

Love – an intense feeling of deep affection, devotion, passion, cherish, delight in, and others. There are many faces of love: for parent, sibling, child, friend, spouse or partner, and humanity as a whole which accepts everything within the disposition of the loved object, good and bad.

Truth – eternal principle of right, or law and order, veracity, fidelity, conformity to rule or example, righteousness, certainty, quality or state of being true. However much truth is hidden in bad deeds, in the end it shall all be revealed, and the "truth shall set you free."

Example: the abuse of children by priests and celebrities over the years came to light in the first quarter of the twenty-first century. And, in the end, truth "sets the good-doers free".

Grace - decorum in conduct, refinement in acquiescence, kindness in selflessness, smoothness and elegance of movement, courtesy in good will, finesse in impressive delicacy and skill, tactful in diplomacy (example: the occasion was graced by their presence).

Charity – the disposition to think well of others, liberality, alms in giving voluntarily to those in need, universal love, altruism, humanitarianism, philanthropy, aid, assistance, compassion and generosity.

Peace is freedom from disturbance, tranquillity at the end of war, free from anxiety or distress, quiet, serenity, tranquillity and harmony.

Justice - rectitude in dealing with others, impartiality, the quality of being just in behaviour or treatment, in other words give just measure to all.

When one ceases to walk in the path of righteousness he/she is under the direction of Satan. As such, one is bound to bring suffering upon him/herself and upon others. When the measure of time allocated for the evil deed has run out Satan ceases to be powerful and the justice of God prevails. So behind the power of time, the importance of planet Earth and the evil of Satan, lies the glory and goodness of God – God reigns supreme.

****

Thoughts on the concept of reward and punishment

I personally do not believe in reward and punishment hereafter, heaven and hell in other words. It is said that we were made 'in the image of God'. This, to me, means spiritually rather than physically and the power and ability bestowed upon us. God is an abstract being, a spirit, and as such the spiritual side of each one of us is part of God. This does not mean the body is of less importance but body and soul are inseparable, each with its own value to enable our passage through planet Earth, for we are in transit.

But the natural law of compensation will operate, understood as Karma in Hinduism and Buddhism.

The meaning is that the sum of a person's actions in this and previous states of existence, viewed as deciding their fate in future existence. In other words good or bad luck, is viewed as resulting from one's actions. I personally do not believe in previous states of existence. Save that on planet Earth we are regenerated over and over again in posterity as we are the posterity of our ancestors.

The English Metaphysical poet Francis Quarles (1592-1644) explains compensation: "As there is no worldly gain without some loss, so there is no worldly loss without some gain. If thou hast lost thy wealth, thou hast lost some trouble with it. If thou are degraded from the honour, thou art likewise freed from the stroke of envy. If sickness hast blurred the beauty, it hath delivered thee from pride. Set the allowance against the loss and thou shall find no loss great."

Two important things are:

a) **Perception** - the ability to see, hear, or become aware of something through the senses.

b) **Discernment** - the ability to judge well.

The two are very important in our journey through life. When we encounter something or someone in life how our relationship will fare depends on our perception and discernment at the outset. If instantly we perceived any shortcomings and we walked away from the situation or person (not condemnation) we could and would avoid disappointment. If we did not walk away from the situation, it was lack of discernment.

On the point of 'reward and punishment', I find that the poem by William Ernest Henley *Invictus* (invincible: Latin meaning 'unconquerable') amply describes the journey of life.

William Ernest Henley's poem *Invictus* analysed:

First stanza: Out of the night that covers me...

[Darkness is a metaphor for evil, and perhaps pessimism]

Black as the pit from pole to pole...

[The blankness covers everything, "the Pit" is Hell, referring to the

North Pole and South Pole of planet Earth, in fact, all over the

world.]

I thank whatever gods may be...

[He is not thanking a particular god, suggestive of several gods of

various believers.]

For my unconquerable soul.

[Whatever physical adversity he faces his soul remains firmly intact.

Second   **In the fell clutch of circumstance...**

stanza: [Fell, bad or evil, cruel or unrelenting control, like a mouse or small

bird in the grip of the claws of a hawk.]

I have not winced nor cried aloud...

[The body may be broken but not the spirit, he did not show any

signs of pain or fear.]

Under the bludgeonings of chance...

[Like being beaten over the head with a club or other blunt

instrument (metaphorically), no anticipation of what would happen.

My head is bloody but unbowed.

[Wounded but will not acknowledge defeat, endure the beating

and never surrender, staunch in the will to survive.]

Third stanza: Beyond this place of wrath and tears...

[Wrath is anger, book of common prayer refers to life as 'the vale

of tears'.]

Looms but the horror of the shade...

[Poetic expression for death, frightening shade is ghost or spook.]

Yet the menace of the years...

[Whatever is bothering him does not scare him, not before, nor in

the future, he will overcome and proceed.]

Finds and shall find me unafraid.

[A spirit that never flinched once even in the face of problems.]

Fourth   **It matters not how strait the gate...**

stanza: [Strait is narrow, Biblical, Matthew 7:13 on Jesus saying the gate to

heaven is narrow, whether created by society or religion to the poet

it is immaterial to the poet.]

Or how charged with punishment the scroll...

[Scroll is the rules and laws created by society which people must

follow, but he is staunch in his own belief and faith in himself.]

I am the master of my fate...

[Recognise no one but yourself as master, for you to earn it, me,

myself, I am responsible for what I do.]

I am the captain of my soul.

[I guide my soul to wherever I want to go, regardless of ups and

downs, wiser and happier will I be in life as I depend upon myself

and my own actions and on no one else's.]

To the above, in my adult life, I added the statement by Jesus in Matthew 14:27, and later quoted by Pope John Paul II, in *Crossing The Threshold of Hope* (1993). A book written with humility and generosity sixteen years into his Papacy and on the eve of the Millennium; his message, quoting Jesus, is simply *"Be not afraid".* Further addition: *"I am with you always."*

About William Ernest Henley:

The poem *Invictus* by Henley was introduced by my father to my brother and I when I was seven years old (1937). This poem has greatly inspired me throughout my life and I have found much strength from it. 'Unconquerable' in the face of trials and tribulations one remains intact.

My father also told us about the man Henley who suffered a tuberculosis infection of the bones when he was in his early twenties that resulted in the amputation of his leg below the knee. His other leg was saved by Dr Joseph Lister (1827-1912), the developer of antiseptic medicine. Henley wrote the poem *Invictus* (and other poems) during his twenty-month ordeal between 1873 and 1875 at the Royal Edinburgh Infirmary in Scotland. Robert Louis Stevenson, his friend, based on Henley the character Long John silver, a peg-legged pirate, in the Stevenson novel *Treasure Island*.

Henley married Hannah (Anna, nee Johnson Boyle - we found this interesting since my mother's name was Hannah and she was called Anna but spelt Anaa) and they had a daughter Margaret who was a sickly child. Margaret died when she was five. She became immortalised as 'Wendy' by J M Barrie in his children's classic *Peter Pan.* He named her Wendy because she could not say 'friend' but 'fwendy'.

****

Ego of the present

Our Founding Fathers were *rooted in the ego of the present*, paid only lip service to the importance of the 'Spirit': the thing of ultimate beauty in a human being, the everlasting substance though intangible by the five senses. They paid much heed to the material world and its contents mainly by politics and commerce. As such our history of the human race is incomplete and lacks key issues.

When I think about the human body and its ephemeral passage through earth, the question that comes to my mind is:

"Can a skilled artist make a beautiful ornament only to smash it in the end?"

(See The Promised Land).

The human body is truly the Creator's beautiful ornament, for every part, every limb a use but its sojourn on earth is brief. The point is that the legacy upon which our understanding of the phenomenal world never conditioned us to think about the brief nature or characteristic of the human body, at the same time the importance of the human body. We were and we are prevented by the ego of the present and fail to ask: Why the brief characteristic of our stay on earth?

The answer is 'regeneration' which applies to all species on earth with varying degrees of the allocation of time of existence. The human body is constantly regenerated: we are the same people who first populated the earth: In Creation, the story of Adam and Eve; in Science and DNA, Mitochondrial Eve and Mitochondrial Adam (see The Veil, chapter 2, Creation or Evolution?). Is Regeneration not Resurrection?

In our constant regeneration our ancestors live on in us and we shall live on in posterity. Even those who never had children, there are the offspring of their siblings or cousins who have the same genes from their common ancestors – the human race is 'one people'.

While everything on earth evolves: the setting; the circumstances, or the outlook of any place; man-made changes; the human body and its inherent needs, character - instincts of hate, love, passion, cruelty, kindness, desires, ambitions, successes, failures and many, many others remain unaltered. This is because we are the same people, in regeneration over and over again through the centuries. Very few people, if at all, are concerned about these factors because we are hooked on materialism – rooted in the ego of the present. This inherent streak is the basis of conflicts and war in our failure to be more considerate to our fellow beings.

The body is not built to last forever like the monuments built by man, even though history proves that much of what man has built over the centuries lies and remains in fossilised form. The body is fragile, and as delicate as the tiny little shrimp in the vast ocean. The body is a tabernacle or temple housing the soul on its temporal journey through the Physical Sphere (see The Veil, Part 3. chapter 7 Ministry of Yeshua, Body).

CHAPTER 7

Major Rescuers:

At my age of four weeks my life commenced on a 'banana leaf' when my grand mother Asaina rescued me (see *Blantyre and Yawo Women,* chapter 8, Farewell Atati, narrated by my mother, Hannah, daughter of Asaina).

The second rescuer was my *pater* (Latin, a person's legal father) Yusof (Joseph) Ishmail when he and my mother got married and he adopted my brother and I (ditto chapter 10, The Fountain).

As indicated in chapter 1 above, on the spiritual aspect when I was eight, I was rescued by Yeshua, the Jew who came to be known as 'Jesus Christ' (see *The Veil; and The Promised Land – Companion to The Veil*). This is the major rescuer "for all time".

In the year 2000 in my twilight years I was rescued by Lorna, my daughter and Archie Leitch, her partner, a Scotsman. The rescue by Lorna and Archie involved my move to Dumfries, Scotland, where 6 weeks after my move I had a mild stroke. At the age of 85 even a mild stroke can be a major trauma in one's life since one is permanently altered in body and spirit. I was rescued by the National Health Service (NHS), particularly the Rehabilitation Unit of the NHS (see *No Man's Land*), what I have called above the 'in-between rescues'.

In 2011 out of the blue came Kelly Ishmail, the son of Yusof (Joseph) Ishmail, to rescue me in more ways than one (see *Blantyre and Yawo Women*, chapter 22, Twenty-first Century). In particular in the management of my assets in Malawi, my homeland, under my Trust for the benefit of the needy, particularly children and the elderly – the most vulnerable in any society.

The above are what I call 'the major rescuers' which I regard as the basis of other rescues in between in given situations, circumstances, and in varying degrees.

When we came to live with *Pater* at Nyambadwe, our home was close to the home of Colonel John Sanders, a retired British colonel of the First World War (see *Blantyre and Yawo Women*, chapter 10, The Fountain). His wife, Mrs Enid Sanders, informally adopted me and I owe much of my British culture to this beautiful English lady, particularly the introduction to English literature by the children's books she gave me.

When I had been imprisoned on trumped up charges the person who fought for me, and in fact, saved my life (perhaps unwittingly) was my defence lawyer, Bright Msaka (see *Blantyre and Yawo Women,* Historical Information, Bantu Invasions and Infusions). He persisted in contacting the Attorney General who ordered that I be released immediately. I had been imprisoned in a small cell at the Blantyre Remand Prison, Malawi, for five hours (see *Blantyre and Yawo Women*, Chapter 20, Definitive Journey).

****

October 2016: The passing of Helen, a special friend

A few days prior to my dream I had sent an email to Helen, telling her of my new telephone number. She did not reply which was most unusual. I repeated my message and still there was no answer. I tried calling her on my WhatsApp mobile phone but mysteriously her number had disappeared from my mobile phone.

Thursday 03 November I was having my daily siesta (6:30-7:00 pm, rather later than usual) and had the following dream:

Helen was walking away from me at a place I had never been to before. The place was sandy with a slight incline which obscured the place she was walking to (see below for my understanding of this place).

I followed her, calling after her but she did not answer me. She carried on walking away as if she was going on some 'urgent mission' and I had the feeling that I was being snubbed.

I called after her again several times, while following her behind, the incline still obscuring where she was going. She turned round and looked at me but continued on her 'mission'.

After several more attempts at calling her, she turned round, again and responded back in time:

> "Your dad is not there, he is in spirit", she said with conviction.
> "What about my mother?" I asked.
> "She is in spirit, too." She replied indifferently and in a dismissive manner.

When I awoke, the dream gave me the now familiar feeling of 'bereavement' and I was upset. I now had the strong feeling to communicate and find out how she was and tried the WhatsApp again but her number was not on my phone. So I telephoned her son to enquire about her. It was he who was dismissive and he was not prepared to tell me what was wrong with his mother. Instead he said:

> "We have blocked all the telephones because we are tired of people calling
> us to enquire about our Mum."

He would not tell me what was wrong with Helen, despite that I was a close friend of the family. I found this to be a reasonable attitude because he felt that the family were being violated somehow and this was understandable to me anyway.

A lawyer mutual friend of Helen and I told me by WhatsApp text that Helen had been diagnosed with cancer around the third week of October 2016. He kept me posted on her condition and so did her lovely daughter-in-law, though I prayed and hoped that this premonition should not be accurate as previous ones and not take effect. Just over five months later (5 months of apprehension), I received a text from our mutual friend. Sadly on Saturday 22 April 2017, at 9 pm my special friend passed on... She was only 7 months older than my daughter (64).

In business Helen was a mogul; in faith she was a pastor; in charity she was monumental and had helped many people particularly women. In her short life she had achieved far more than most people achieve in a lifetime (see *Blantyre and Yawo Women*, chapter 11).

A leader who was affluent, by sheer hard work throughout her life, would not rob the people in any way. She was the hope for a better future for Malawi. She would have steered the country away from its appalling current abject poverty because of selfish leadership – she was going to stand for president in 2019.

Why did she die so young? Why do some people die when they are so young? In death there is 'absolute equality', for death knows no age, rank or any of the distinctions and man-made barriers that separate people. But 'death' is something that applies only to the body, at least that is my belief - we simply transfer to the Spiritual Sphere, a place of eternal life, the place beyond.

There is another answer to this question. In the Spiritual Sphere (SS) some can influence progress in a particular field in the Physical Sphere and examples of this abound (see The Spiritual Sphere below).

My interpretation of this dream:

The dream was a positive message of death to me. However, the setting of the place of the dream calls for clarification. Sand is a naturally occurring granular material composed of finely divided rock and mineral particles, weathered from inland rocks and transported to the beach. It is also precipitated out of the ocean water by marine organism. A variety of time-scales are recorded in sand. Some say that sand represents or signifies *dead sea* from what once was part of the sea. Dead sea describes our planet Earth that it is a place of death and decay which Helen was leaving behind for the 'Spiritual Sphere'.

The slight incline obscured Helen's destination because no one really knows where we go when we die and what exactly 'eternity' is, and our thoughts about eternity are just a hunch.

Although in the dream I was following behind Helen as fast as I could walk, yet somehow, I could not progress to where she was at. My feet were up to just below the sandy incline, and touched only a very small section of it. I interpret this to mean that not immediately but imminently, I shall be following those who passed on before me to the place beyond. This message came to me in a strong conviction in the song *Mississippi* by its music and lyrics (I have indicated above how music and lyrics brought messages to me).

16 June 2017 - A personal message was clear to me in the tune 'Mississippi' (by Pussycat) which suddenly came to me on the above date (I listen to music while working on my computer) giving details of my departure for *The Place Beyond*. This departure could be in one or either, of two ways: shutting down of my body because it is unable to continue (due to severe osteoarthritis) or departure of the soul and spirit – see chapter 5 above, *A Wake Up Call*.

The tune transformed me into that sad feeling (which I have analysed below) - separations are always heart-rending. My passing on, as I have indicated above, does not affect me as much as the passing on of others. In fact, I look upon my departure from planet Earth with some euphoria.

The most significant aspect of the song is that it portrays my belief that life is a river whose waters forever pass away...

"Mississippi"

   Well you can hear the country song from far,
   And someone plays the honky tonky guitar,
   Where all the lights will go on one by one,
   People enjoying the sun,
   And the wind takes it away,
   Where the Mississippi rolls down to the sea,
   And lovers found the place they like to be.
   How many times before this song was ending,
   Love and understanding everywhere around.

The above words indicate the *status quo* (Latin the state in which things are). This may apply to a *status quo* of any people in any part of the world, to change by the tide of time as the "...wind takes it away..."

Life is a river that remains as a permanent feature of the terrain of the area but the water that rolls through it is in constant change; in other words, not the same water rolling down to the sea. The water represents 'people' passing on yet constantly regenerated by the birth of new people...bringing in current ideals..."where the Mississippi rolls down to the sea..." the water...in other words people dispersed into the sea.

> Mississippi, I'll remember you,
> Whenever I shall go away,
> I'll be longing for the day,
> When I will be in Greenville again,
> Mississippi you'll be on my mind,
> Every time I hear this song,
> Mississippi rolls along until the end of time.

'Greenville' refers to a town in Mississippi. The song indicates a hope to be there again, suggestive of happiness experienced in 'Greenville'. Therefore Greenville could be in any part of the world where one has known happiness and tranquillity. We do not know what we do when we have passed on to the place beyond. "I always will be calling"... Do we look back on planet Earth to reflect upon our happy experiences there - "Dreams of yesterday?" I believe that at the place beyond we can see and perceive all on planet Earth though those on Earth do not have the same ability or capacity.

We remember something that has passed on, longing to return to what has been good but knowing that the river will roll on till the end of time...

> Now the country song forever lost its soul,
> When the guitar player turns to rock'n'roll,
> And every time when summer nights are falling,
> I always will be calling, dreams of yesterday.

Seemingly the guitar player is the same one who played the "country song" and only the genre of the tune has changed but in fact it is not the same guitar player in the 'new water' rolling in the river...constant change brings novelty... "the country song" forever transformed into "rock 'n' roll", the current ideal, or the *status quo*, to evolve again in renewed water forever... The dreams of yesterday brings back pleasant memories...

>Mississippi, I'll remember you,
>Whenever I shall go away,
>I'll be longing for the day,
>When I will be in Greenville again,
>Mississippi you'll be on my mind,
>Every time I hear this song,
>Mississippi rolls along until the end of time...
>Every time I hear this song,
>Mississippi rolls along until the end of time.

In all Spheres of existence, the Physical and Spiritual, there is no end of time, hence "until the end of time" is a metaphor.

CHAPTER 8

The Spiritual Sphere

The state of the Spiritual Sphere does not mean it operates only after death but the state of mind determines the sphere of the spirit; whether it is in the Physical or Spiritual Spheres, that state should be considered as the sphere in which the spirit lives.

The baby in mother's arms has no other sphere for the time being than that of physical life until after development in growth of the spirit. (Though according to my belief, the personal spirit is there from the moment of conception.) Therefore, the first sphere is one of selfishness: grasp for food, cry aloud when in pain, and knows nothing of the broader region. The selfishness or the ego from the moment of birth is present throughout life in varying degrees according to the individual.

In Creation are dual aspects, its internal character and external form, and positive and negative elements. The internal character is invisible to the five senses of the body and beyond the reach of scientific instruments, and it is responsible for the behaviour of the external reality that is visible. This has left its study to the area of religion which is the object of much scepticism in the modern scientific world, though science recognises the existence of the invisible causal forces.

The founding fathers in religion were too concerned with the material world of commerce and politics by which the reality or purpose of religion was lost. There are many Christian denominations today, like other religions, whereby the leaders operate them like 'businesses' where-from they draw salaries and some become wealthy. God is not a piece of merchandise to be vended. The Roman Catholic Church itself, claims to have originated with Christ (two hundred years after his death!) and the apostles as the oldest church: "Holy Mother Church" (in Latin *"Sancta Mater Ecclesia"*), and is one of the wealthiest institutions on earth.

****

Although I have known many trials and tribulations in my life, there have always been rescuers and I consider myself very fortunate. I believe that Jesus in the Spiritual Sphere influenced people in the Physical Sphere to rescue me over the years. When others pass on into the Spiritual Sphere they can influence certain people in particular aspects in the Physical Sphere. There is overwhelming evidence on this point. The following are just a few examples of leaders who after they moved on into the Spiritual Sphere their ideals lived on through certain people in the Physical Sphere.

Dr David Livingstone, the Scottish explorer (1813-1873)

Although Dr David Livingstone arrived on the shore of Nyasa (lake) on 17 September 1859, and despite his famous appeal in his Cambridge lectures of 1857, it was not until after his death (1 May 1873, at Chitambo, Zambia) that his torch was carried forward in his plea to replace the slave trade with Christianity and Commerce. The return of his body to Britain in 1874 and his funeral in Westminster Abbey triggered new interest in Nyasaland (now Malawi). The Free Church of Scotland (Free Church Mission) arrived in 1875 and was called Livingstonia Mission. Also the Church of Scotland (the Church of Scotland Mission) decided to send missions to Malawi in 1876 in honour of Livingstone. Its first station was named Blantyre, around which the modern city of Blantyre later developed – Blantyre, Glasgow, Lanarkshire, the birth place of Livingstone.

Mahatma Gandhi (1869-1948) – the most famous of the world's peaceful political dissidents

A 'non-violent' civil disobedience activist for the independence of India from Britain, about whom most historians say more than anything else Gandhi proved that one man has the power to take on an empire using both ethics and intelligence. He inspired movements for civil rights and freedom across the world well after his death.

Martin Luther King Jr - "I Have A Dream" - (1928-1969)

American Baptist minister and activist who became the most visible spokesperson and leader in the Civil Rights Movement. Martin's dream described a vision of racial equality in America inspiring millions. Despite provocation, he remained true to the motto of 'non-violent'. He used the tactics of non-violent and civil disobedient based on his Christian beliefs. He was inspired by Gandhi and argued that Gandhi's philosophy was "the only morally and practically sound method open to oppressed people in their struggle for freedom". Luther attributed Gandhi's ideas of non-violent direct action in the larger framework of Christianity, declaring that Christ showed us the way and Gandhi in India showed it could work.

The entire culture of later generation in various fields is inspired and based upon the ideals, vision, and actions of bygone pioneers whose legacy lives on.

Epilogue

Blood Groups

EVERYBODY'S BLOOD LOOKS THE SAME: 'red fluid', but there are very important distinctions. In the ABO system blood can be divided in four main groups: A, B, AB, and O. The surface of the cells in each group is different and will act as an antigen to plasma from another group, which carries the antibody. Group A cells will carry the antibody B in the plasma. Those in group AB do not carry either antibody, while those in group O have both antibodies but the cells do not have either antigen. Antibody is a blood protein produced in response to and counteracting a specific antigen. Antibodies combine chemically with substances which the body recognizes as alien, such as bacteria, viruses, and foreign substances in the blood.

Thousands of lives are saved by blood transfusions but they could be disastrous if the blood groups of donor and recipient were not compatible. The ABO and Rhesus factor antigens are very important in deciding which blood type someone should receive. Rh negative blood is regarded as the most precious blood on earth for people with very rare types. Obtaining lifesaving blood can involve a complex network of donors and doctors that stretches across the world. Within the ABO system people with blood group O are called universal donors, because their blood does not contain antigens. This means their blood can be given to anyone, irrespective of blood group. People with blood group AB are the universal recipients who can receive any blood group, because they do not make antibodies to antigens of A or B.

At birth the placenta separates from the uterus wall and a limited amount of mixing may occur. An RhD Negative mother may have an RhD Positive child and at birth mother may receive some of the baby's blood and may hence become sensitised to it. To stop an immune response developing, she would be given an anti-D injection promptly to destroy the red cells with the rhesus antigen. This was a scientific development since the early 1960s. The anti-

D injection will "mop up" any rhesus positive antigens, preventing production of antibodies against the baby; and it reduces the risk of an RhD Negative mother becoming sensitised. Prior to this the foetus died in the womb or soon after birth. If the mother develops anti-D antibodies and later had another RhD Positive child, her immune response to it could cause damage to the child. The foetal blood develops uniquely and individually and there is the danger of possible mixing of mother's and blood of the foetus. Now advanced nations know their own ABO blood group (A, B, O, or AB) and most also know whether they are Rh Positive or Rh Negative. This means that now a foetus or a baby no longer dies unnecessarily.

The Rhesus system is named after the Rhesus monkey, following experiments by Karl Landsteiner and Alexander S Wiener; and only five percent of the world population of 7 billion (census of 2013) have Rhesus Negative blood. The RhD Negative Factor has baffled scientists, and until today science has no explanation as to where the RhD Negative blood originated from. The problem arises when a mother has Rh Negative blood and father with Rh Positive and they produce a baby with Rh Positive blood. The RhD Negative blood of mother, carrying an RhD Positive blood child, rejects her own offspring. If two Rh Negatives try to have a baby, where pregnancy goes full term the baby will usually die or be born a 'blue' baby (which some have erroneously referred to as royal blood) because it is not processing oxygen properly; and the baby becomes jaundiced soon after birth. The RhD Negative blood Factor is a subject that has inspired many researchers and writers. But any attempt to explain the origin of this mystery can only be mere assumptions or speculations to this day.

The ancient texts hold many stories, particularly pre-Christian texts, about beings with other worldly blood that came to earth from the heavens and created man or a kind of man in their image. They were regarded as gods by man, they lived long lives and performed miracles. Some connect Rhesus Negative blood to Biblical explanations, and that the RhD Negative Factor is not of the Earth. And, that it originated with the Elohim family godhead who were not permitted to marry and bear children with any other than their own blood type. On the Biblical aspect, Daniel 2:43(KJV) says:

"...they will mingle with the seed of men; but they will not adhere to one another; just as iron does not mix with clay."

It is also speculated that RhD Negative blood may have been caused by some sort of mutation that occurred many thousands of years ago. It is possible that the original humans created by the Old Testament god, with RhD Positive blood, have been altered by extraterrestrials affiliated with the New Testament god, resulting in mutation of DNA and deletion of the RhD Positive factor, producing RhD Negative blood, according to Stanley Karnow author of *In Our Image*. He quotes Luke's gospel as going through the genealogy backward in time listing the generations and ends with "...the son of Seth, the son of Adam, the son of God'. He suggests that Adam was the son of God, hence DNA of the father in the god of the Old Testament. He asks that Adam and all his descendants would they not have RhD Negative blood? But who holds the true answer to this? In my belief, God is an "all-embracing Spirit" who is above the "physical aspect", then how could the Almighty pass blood of any type to anyone? (Note: I prefer to use 'Almighty' for pronoun of God, for God is neither male nor female.)

Scientists and people who are interested in the Rhesus Factor, have all sorts of theories: some say RhD Negative blood is blue blood or royal blood. My view is that on planet Earth there can be no blue or royal blood, these are man-made eulogies which create distinctions or differences that separate people – a matter of social conditioning: all people are one. Furthermore, the issue of RhD Negative is shrouded by 'importance' in the ego of the present; and the view of 'blue' or 'royal blood' is a wrong track which prevents scientists from discovering the real truth about RhD Negative blood – set aside the importance and in all humility seek the truth.

****

The Mystery of RhD Negative Blood – Genetic Origin Unknown

RhD Positive blood can be traced to the Rhesus monkey and all other primates, but RhD Negative blood is not. In fact, it cannot be traced anywhere else in nature. Also RhD Positive blood can be cloned but RhD Negative blood cannot be cloned. It would seem that RhD Negative affects more women, and babies, and less men.

In my own researches and according to my own experience and the experience of others I have spoken to on this subject, particularly two others, Salma Khan, my grand niece, granddaughter of my brother, Cader; and Izabela Brzezinska a young Polish woman who adopted me as her grandmother, I discovered a number of things connected to people with RhD Negative blood, aside from the fact that mother's own blood kills her baby. These findings include the following:

A feeling of not belonging – throughout my life I experienced this, particular with my own family and I always felt that I did not belong – I am more comfortable with people who are not members of my family.

Sense of a "Mission" in life – I have always felt a sense of mission and that my mission was to help others when they were in need. On the few occasions I was unable to help for whatever reason, I suffered and do suffer much regret.

An extra rib or vertebra. I have an extra vertebra in my spinal column.

Higher than average IQ – Salma and Izabela (mentioned above) both are of higher than average IQ.

Love of Space & Science – I love space but much of science fiction movies put me off science though two movies that impressed me most were science fiction: *The Time Machine* (the original 1960 movie with Rod Taylor) and *E.T. The Extraterrestrial.* [I am thinking about writing a science fiction novel on the phasing out of the aeroplane in future travel, if I can make it as I am almost at the end of my twilight years now.]

Love of Space & Science – I love space but much of science fiction movies put me off though two movies that impressed me most were science fiction: *The Time Machine* and *E.T. The Extraterrestrial*. [I am thinking about writing a science fiction novel on the phasing out of the aeroplane in future travel, if I can make it as I am almost at the end of my twilight years now.]

More sensitive vision & other senses – I have a sensitive vision and other senses. This may be compared to a deaf person who is susceptible to a perceptual illusion that hearing people do not experience; or the intuition of a person who is blind.

Increased sensitivity to heat & sunlight – this applies to me, heat affects me, particularly from the sun (to the extent of suffering from sunstroke on 2 occasions, ironically one in Scotland and another in England but never in sunny Africa) and sunlight affects my eyes.

Psychic abilities - the scientific definition refers to those abilities to perceive things about the world through a "sixth sense". This is why types of psychic abilities are referred to as extrasensory perception (*The Place Beyond* is on psychic abilities). Psychic Dreams and/or increased psychic and intuitive abilities. I recalled how my faculties could grasp and understand inexplicable natural laws. Particularly on dreams, it was true that I was and I am often guided by esoteric dreams. I have always dreamed much, and still do, often about incidents that were to occur, before they occurred.

From the age of eight I had dreamed of important events to come and when I tried to explain to others about my dreams, I was told that I was weird. My dreams had upset my mother and she told me that "I was not normal". From then on, I had decided to keep my dreams to myself.

Truth seekers – I believe that truth always comes out in the end, no matter how hard one tries to conceal it. In recent years it became more and more apparent that some priests and certain celebrities had over the years sexually abused children (see *The Veil*, chapter 10, New Covenant and Administration of the Church, At the Hands of Wardens). I also believe that "the truth shall set you free."

Predominantly blue, green, or Hazel eyes – this does not apply to me though it may apply to others.

Low body temperature – is where blood pressure in one's arteries is abnormally low when the blood vessels in hands, feet, arms, and legs start to get narrower, leading to hypothermia. This applies to me (though I have managed to avoid a state of hypothermia).

Piercing eyes – look, gaze, etc describes the fact of a person looking very carefully at someone or something especially when they are trying to discover something often making people feel uncomfortable. Sometimes I find myself in this situation and I have to keep reminding myself not to do this.

Empathetic Illnesses – are those in which you manifest symptoms that are not your own. Agoraphobic with panic disorders, chronic depression, fatigue, pain or mysterious ailments. These apply to me except depression in any form, no matter how difficult a situation may be I have not found myself depressed.

Ability to disrupt electrical devices – this does not apply to me.

Red or reddish tint to hair colour – hairdressers have said to me: "There are red lights in in your black hair", though now no more as my hair is almost all grey.

Prone to Alien Abductions – Professor Rich McNally and his colleagues at Harvard University over a period of 10 years researched the psychology of alien abductees, and in particular why was it that some people embrace the identify of 'alien abductees'. He argues that each of the claimants contributes to the experiences when they recalled being abducted and indicated a desire to cling to their beliefs. I have never been abducted by aliens! I personally do not believe that there are aliens, save that there are people among us who have characteristics that are unlike the majority; and it is typical of human nature to regard what is 'different' as alien.

Experience unexplained phenomenon – when with my parents as a child we lived in a haunted house, I was able to feel and see things which the members of my family did not, though they said the house was haunted. When we left that house the new tenants confirmed strange things that happened in that house which were similar to what I had experienced, that was seen and heard.

Allergic to medication and certain types of food -

During most of my life I had been allergic to certain kinds of medication, and certain kinds of food, the reasons for which at the time I did not and could not understand. My body could reject them immediately or within half an hour at the most. This would manifest by bleeding from the nose, ears, and mouth. In some instances I would get what seemingly was a water infection in my urine, though tests carried out could not find any infection; or diarrhoea, accompanied by a flow of blood, but very rarely vomiting, though a blood-flow from my mouth, as evidenced on my pillow and bed linen.

On food, I monitored myself on my body's reaction to the foods I ate; and by trial and error I was able to pin-point those items which did not agree with me and eliminated them from my menu. I came to understand the values contained in food, some friendly and others not. It is said: 'one man's food is poison to another'. Consequently I had become selective on what I ate over the years (see *Enduring Fountain – Health and Wellbeing*). I met doctors and nutritionists for various information, and reading books on the subject; and came to realise that whenever I bled it was my body's own way of cleansing itself from what it considered the medication or food as an antigen to itself. It became clear to me that this was evidenced by the bleeding of my navel when I was deliberately poisoned by milk.

Empathy & Compassion for Mankind: on my feelings towards others, I recalled several instances when I had been understanding to other people. This aspect of feelings towards 'another', I discovered, had been extended to domestic animals, and some wild. Throughout my life, from childhood, I have been and I am able to communicate with animals, and birds.

Mysterious - I also realised that I was less understandable to other people. More often than not I had been reminded by certain people that they found it difficult or impossible to understand me.

Deep thinker - I am a deep thinker, even in the company of other people, I fight to ensure that I am with the rest of them, as I am liable to be thinking deeply about something in the presence of others, and as such I have been referred to as "absent minded".

Youth - the ability to tap the fountain of youth. I had maintained my youth beyond age eighty and more often than not people generally were unable to tell my real age (see *Enduring Fountain – Health and Well-being*).

Rh Negative Blood - Tend to be Healers – I do not claim to be a healer though I am interested in alternative medicine upon which I have survived from most ailments for many years, and believe that all societies are gifted with the ability to heal the sick according to their culture (see *Enduring Fountain – Health and Well-being*).

****

Immortal Infants

FIVE MONTHS AFTER MY MARRIAGE, I had felt as if I was carrying some heavy load; a strange and indescribable feeling came over me, completely transforming my mind, and my body became strange and alien to me. Three weeks after this feeling it was confirmed that I was pregnant.

Francis, my husband the father, selected the names saying:

"If its a boy, he shall be named Basil; and if a girl she shall be named Lorna.

At eight weeks of my pregnancy I felt an unexplainable tiredness and my legs seemed to give way. About midnight I experienced severe abdominal pain, then I began to haemorrhage and by morning I had miscarried. I was devastated. The doctor had assured me that there would be other pregnancies and there was nothing to worry about.

****

FIVE MONTHS LATER I HAD SIMILAR SIMPTOMS, that of 'transforming my mind and body', my second pregnancy was confirmed. There were no complications throughout the nine months of gestation. I first felt persistent lower back pain combined with abdominal pain, like pre-menstrual feeling and cramps. Followed by painful contractions occurring at regular and increasingly shorter intervals. With a gush my waters broke and I was taken to the home of our family GP. My baby Lorna, who is RhD Positive like her father, was born perfect without any complications (see *Journey of Discovery*).

The allergic reaction is when an RhD Negative blood mother is carrying an RhD Positive blood child. Her blood builds up antibodies to destroy an alien substance (the same way it would a virus), thereby destroying the infant. How come then that Lorna not only survived but she was perfect in every way? In short, she was not destroyed.

This successful birth may be attributed to the fact that my mother Hannah, and my grandmother, Asaina, had obtained a woman herbalist to protect my pregnancy. The herbalist prepared *mbande* (in the Yawo language), a square measuring about three inches long by three inches wide; made from cloth within which medicine was sewn. This was attached to a medicated piece of string to fit my waistline loosely and I was to wear it throughout the pregnancy without ever removing it once not even when I was having a bath, until the day the baby was to be born. The herbalist declined to receive any payment and said:

"I cannot take payment until this woman gives birth to a healthy baby." Sadly, at that time I never explored the nature of the medication that was used, and I remain ignorant of what I now consider to be an important factor because I strongly believe that my baby Lorna was saved by the woman herbalist.

****

SIX MONTHS LATER I HAD SIMILAR SIMPTOMS, that of

'transforming my mind and body', and my third pregnancy was confirmed. All had been complacent in the belief that all was well and would be well, since Lorna was born perfect, and the herbalist was never asked to protect the pregnancy. There appeared to be no complications throughout the nine months of gestation. It was decided by the doctor who delivered Lorna and consented to by my parents that the birth could take place at my parents' home.

The doctor sent to my parents' home the same midwife who delivered Lorna a couple of days before the birth of the baby. I had the similar persistent lower back pain combined with abdominal pain, like pre-menstrual feeling and cramp; followed by painful contractions occurring at regular and increasingly shorter intervals. With a gush my waters broke and the doctor was sent for. The baby was blue at birth and arrived with the cord intertwined round his neck. The midwife was skilful and untangled the cord but there was no sound. She held him by the legs, head down, it was a tense moment, baby normally enters the world with a vibrant cry in the overwhelming intake of air. The midwife smacked his bottom several times before he gave a cry. He appeared to be normal.

Twenty-four hours later complications developed. He became jaundiced and the doctor gave him a teaspoonful of castor oil. Baby was in great discomfort. Many things went through my mind: Why did baby turn blue before the cry? Why did it take so long for him to cry? Was a teaspoon full of castor oil too much for a Baby's little delicate tummy? Or was there some other mysterious cause? There appeared to be no proper medical knowledge for this condition. After three days baby developed diarrhoea and vomiting, amid much suffering. As I was holding him, he looked with his pleading eyes directly into my eyes, and I read in them: "Help me! Help me! Seeped and surrounded in total ignorance, there was nothing I could do. This went on till after midnight and he seemed to quieten down when I laid him in his cot. Next morning he was gasping for breath, then I picked him up. Four days old, little Joseph passed on to immortality while I was holding him.

****

MY FOURTH PREGNANCY was confirmed, everything appeared to be normal, and yet again, the woman herbalist was never asked to protect the pregnancy. There were no complications till a few days before Baby was due to be born. I felt no movement in my womb, like I was carrying a lump of rock – strangely silent. I was taken to the hospital and was first attended to by a nurse who examined me but said nothing. The look in the nurse's eyes and her silence, save to say:

"The doctor will be with you soon", made me feel uncomfortable.

When the doctor arrived and examined me, he too was strangely quiet. Then I was moved to say:

"I feel no movement at all."

"Me too", he said patting me gently. He came again the following day to say that he would induce labour. It took a whole week, of indescribable grief, before the medics decided to induce labour. I was in agony. A woman hospital cleaner could not resist, she set aside her mop and bucket and came to my aid, opposite to where the doctor was standing. She held my hand. In her comforting gesture, her grip on my hand was strong but gentle. It was a breech birth. Baby was wedged in my pelvis with the buttocks and feet first as opposed to the normal head first delivery.

Baby came right foot first; then in a few minutes, the left foot; and then the rest of the body. When it was over, I asked:

"Is it a girl or a boy?"

"Girl", the doctor replied.

Little Natalie, never completed her journey to Earth – within the womb she passed on to immortality.

This was followed by the visit of a Roman Catholic priest to offer spiritual comfort. Biblically, one would say that since I had carried the first foetus for eight weeks, that was thousands of years. I had held the third baby for four days, that was four thousand years; and I had nurtured the fourth baby in the womb for nine months, that was thousands of years. In the Bible (King James Version) 2 Peter 3:8 reads:

"But do not forget this one thing...with the Lord a day is like a thousand years, and a thousand years are like a day..."

Giving birth to a stillborn baby was horrendous but the mental anguish was worse. I became "over-protective" of Lorna as each day I feared losing her as well. Despite that I had been visited by a friend who was a nursery school teacher, when I was forbidding two-year old Lorna to come down the front steps of my parents' home the friend spoke to me with the strongest conviction:

"Stop what you are doing! Do you want Lorna to be a weakling?"

I questioned myself if I had been fair to Lorna, but it was not till after ten years that I picked myself up and began to live in the strong belief that I had much to live for, Lorna...

During these trials and tribulations my parents were most supportive, they remained a "tower of strength"; and they looked after Lorna very well. For several years after the *immortal infants*, I believed myself to be 'abnormal'; for the evidence of the RhD Negative Factor came in the aftermath. However, I should point out that after the fourth infant, I found consolation in helping others. There were four girls who wanted to study nursing in Britain and I made all the arrangements with Amersham General Hospital, in Buckinghamshire, United Kingdom. This included booking their fares and buying their tickets from the money of our Women's Welfare Association that had become defunct (see *Blantyre and Yawo Women,* chapter 13, Under the Federation of Rhodesia and Nyasaland).

www.ingramcontent.com/pod-product-compliance
Lightning Source LLC
Chambersburg PA
CBHW070134100426
42744CB00009B/1834